YOUR KNOWLEDGE HAS VALUE

Bibliographic information published by the German National Library:

The German National Library lists this publication in the National Bibliography; detailed bibliographic data are available on the Internet at http://dnb.dnb.de .

Imprint:

Copyright © 2012 GRIN Verlag, Open Publishing GmbH
Print and binding: Books on Demand GmbH, Norderstedt Germany
ISBN: 978-3-668-14768-3

This book at GRIN:

http://www.grin.com/en/e-book/195946/book-review-of-the-next-global-stage-challenges-and-opportunities-in

Emmanuel Tete Darko

Book Review of "The Next Global Stage: Challenges and Opportunities in Our Borderless World" (Kenichi Ohmae)

GRIN Publishing

GRIN - Your knowledge has value

Since its foundation in 1998, GRIN has specialized in publishing academic texts by students, college teachers and other academics as e-book and printed book. The website www.grin.com is an ideal platform for presenting term papers, final papers, scientific essays, dissertations and specialist books.

REVIEW OF 'THE NEXT GLOBAL STAGE'

Content

Foreword

The scale of fascinating is in gargantuan proportion in respect to one scholar Fritjof, Capra (2002), contending that global capitalism contrast sharply with ecological sustainability and another scholar Kenichi, Ohmae (2005) also asserting that cross border alliance is the way forward for entrepreneurs (predominantly capitalist) to survive. This is not in any measureable terms to suggest that there is clash of scholarly ideas from two great scholars.

Any firm that aspires to industry leadership in the 21st century must think in terms of global, not domestic, market leadership. The world economy is globalizing at an accelerating pace as countries previously closed to foreign companies open up their markets, as internet shrinks the importance of geographic space, as ambitious growth-minded companies race to build stronger competitive positions in the market of more and more countries.

Firms in industries that are already globally competitive, or in the process of becoming so are under the gun to come up with a strategy for competing successfully in global markets. In all of this, the crucial strategic issues unique to competing across national boundaries are: whether to customize the firm's offerings in each different country market to match the taste and preferences of local buyers or offer a most standardized product globally; whether to employ essentially the same basic competitive strategy in all countries or modify the strategy nation by nation to fit the specific market conditions and competitive circumstances it encounters; where to locate the firm's production facilities, distribution centers and customer service operations so as to realize the greatest locational advantages; and whether and how to efficiently transfer the firm's resource strengths and capabilities from one country to another in an effort to secure competitive edge.

The purpose of this essay is to appraise the works of Kenichi (2005). The Next Global Stage: Challenges and Opportunities in Our Borderless World.

The focus of the literature will be section one; where foreword and biography of the author will be highlighted, section two will stipulate the reviewer's description about the book, objectives of the author, the theme of the book and the author's style and method as well as the book's design. Section three will concentrate on matters arising from the book. The spotlight of section four will be the reviewer's critique about the book, the strengths and weaknesses of the book, the extent to which the book achieved its goals and the impact of the book on the reviewer's life and surroundings and finally a conclusion will be drawn.

1

Biography of The Author

"Kenichi Ohmae, one of world's leading business and corporate strategists, born in 1943 has written over 100 books, including The Mind of the Strategist, The Borderless World, The End of the Nation State, and The Invisible Continent. After earning a doctorate in nuclear engineering from MIT and working as a senior design engineer for Hitachi, he joined McKinsey & Company, rising to senior partner where he led the firm's Japan and Asia Pacific operations. Ohmae currently manages a number of companies that he founded, including Business Breakthrough (a distance learning platform for management education), EveryD.com (a click-and-mortar grocery delivery platform), and Dalian Neusoft Information Services (a BPO platform for data entry in double-bite languages). He is Chancellor's Professor of Public Policy at UCLA, Distinguished Visiting Professor of Korea University and Professor Emeritus at Ewha Women's University in Korea, Trustee and Adjunct Professor of Bond University in Australia, as well as Dean of Kenichi Ohmae Graduate School of Management of BBT University in Japan. In September 2002, he was named the advisor of Liaoning Province and Tianjin City in China" Kenichi, (2005)

Description of The Book by Reviewer

This enthralling book, The Next Global Stage: Challenges and Opportunities in Our Borderless World, the first edition by Kenichi Ohmae (March 27th, 2005). Published by Pearson Prentice Hall and printed in the USA. It contains 282 pages, and was extensively edited by the following personalities: Tim Moore (Editor in Chief); Richard Winkler (Editorial Assistant); Russ Hall (Development Editor); Gina Kanouse (Managing Editor); Sarah Kearns (Senior Project Editor); Krista Hansing (Copy Editor); the cover was designed and cover photograph were crafted by Chuti Prasetsith and Karen Beard correspondingly.

Emphasis should be placed on the fact that Martin Litkowski and Tim Galligan were the marketing manager and international marketing managers respectively

Kenichi Ohmae (2005). "The Next Global Stage" is divided into three parts. Part one encapsulates the stage and has three chapters notably: the world tour; opening night; and the end of economics covering chapters 1, 2 and 3 correspondingly. Part two comprises stage directions and includes four chapters namely: playmakers, platforms for progress, out and about as well as breaking the chains covering chapters 4, 5,6and 7 respectively. Part three encompasses the script and is also made up of four chapters. That is chapters 8, 9, 10 and 11; and envelops reinventing government, the futures market, the next stage and postscript in that order.

The quality of paper used in printing was fabulous and there is considerable good font size with that enhances legibility; with the book's binding being hard cover, durability is assured. It also has accurate index.

Imperatively, the book has the approved seal of Wharton School University of Pennsylvania

Objectives of The Author (Book)

The objective(s) of Kenichi Ohmae (2005) "The Next Global Stage" is to explain what is really happening there in business and politics and provides a script to negotiate a route through the shifting plot lines as well as offering a blueprint for businesses, governments, and individuals who intends to thrive in this new environment. It is edifying to contend that "the Next Global Stage" was shaped by two forces; first it bears witness to changing circumstances and second it witnesses some pioneers of the global economy firsthand.

Kenichi extensive travels round the globe and first hand interaction with people from diverse background which changed his perspectives entirely about business and society was the motivating factor in writing this book.

The Theme of The Book

The theme of Kenichi Ohmae (2005) "The Next Global Stage," is focused on the process of understanding the new rules that apply in this world — and often, there aren't rules to adequately explain what we now experience on a daily basis. This book according to Kenichi Ohmae is not an endpoint nor is it a beginning, but he hopes it is an important step forward for companies and individuals as well as regional and national leaders.

The Author's Method And The Book's Design

Kenichi's was logical and showed proficiency in style on the subject matter that he dealt with and this indeed was a novel. He made use of exact technical expressions to a larger extent, especially when he illustrated how Finland made it great to the top with incessant innovation and investment in research and development in page 14 of his book.

Kenichi extensively acknowledged all those in diverse ways that offered stimulating, enriching but challenging discussions with him that necessitated the birth of this book. He also provided detailed bibliography of sources he referenced and relied heavily on illustrations and circumstances in articulating his points.

Kenichi's style of presentation is simple and logical, but suitable to the subject, readers and the purpose of the author. This book is pregnant with lot of illustrations, statistics, tables, curves, maps, charts and diagrams and these appeals to the five senses of its readers and facilitates blatant understanding.

He resorted to the combination of dialogue, discussions, exposition, narration and descriptions as his method of presentation and is evident in the manner he chronicled his travelled expeditions and the impact it had on people by transforming their view point particularly the business executives. For instance he claimed to have travelled with between 40 and 60 Japanese business executives to witness for themselves 'first hand regions that are attracting money from the rest of the world. And also sending groups of people to Ireland to see how cross border business process outsourcing is reshaping the economy'. Also his commentary of events about the Riverdance at the Great Hall of the People of China and his tour to the city of Dilian near peninsular, these among other scenarios depict his writing style.

Astonishing, Kenichi was extremely critical of the economic theories of astute economist; including Jack Phillips, Keynes, Alfred Marshall, Paul Samuelson, David Ricardo and Adam Smith

Matters Arising From The Book

Kenichi Ohmae (2005) believed that "nothing is more important than actually visiting a place, meeting with companies, and talking to stake holders shows how you develop a feel for what is going on".

It is imperative to underscore that Kenichi made several important arguments that will stimulates mind for years to come. Notably among them are: Business decisions must be considered in terms of four dimensions in today's borderless world: communications, capital, corporations and consumers. He posited that the 4C's have made global economy a true reality since they have the capacity to break all barriers to this concept. This new perspective replaces his famous three C's in The Mind of the Strategist (competitors, the company and consumers).

According to him "the proper geographical entity to consider for decision making is a region rather than a nation state or a trading bloc. Such an entity will usually have at least 10 million

4

people in it and will usually be part of a country; competitiveness is enhanced by expanding up and adding more common platforms (such as Windows, the Web, English, credit card systems, influential paradigms, and parallel educational backgrounds) whether as a company or as a geographical region; paradigms for making national political and economic policy are obsolete because they do not encompass solutions and money flows involving other countries; the new reality is here, but the paradigms to address the reality are not; the borderless world has changed the tasks of political and business leaders in ways that most leaders are ignoring to their peril; the book is enriched by a variety of perspectives involving geographic regions and countries that have prospered where success could not be assumed (such as companies in Sweden, Finland, Singapore, Dalian in China, the Multimedia Super Corridor in Malaysia, and Ireland) and which regions have the potential to become such prosperity centers in the future (especially in Asia and the Baltic)".

Kenichi used the performance of the 'Riverdance' to illustrate the imperatives of how individuals, corporations, and nations survive on interdependency irrespectively of the opulence and or poverty of one. A lucid testimony of this is when developed economies offer colossal proportions of grants, loans, donations and technology to under developed and emerging economies with the view to accelerating the developmental interventions in such disadvantaged economies and in return tapping finite resources (raw materials) from the underdeveloped and emerging economies also to meet their insatiable needs.

Another point worth noting is the credence Kenichi placed on effective branding, customer response and differentiation as winning marketing strategies that offer competitive edge over rivals in page 12 of his book, as very crucial in an attempt to win at the marketplace.

Insightfully, Kenichi demonstrates in pages 13-15 of his book how objectionable and irrelevant it is, not to progress on the root of physical location. This is because technology (internet) has facilitated cross border value added activities. For example the use of the web and powerful search engines plus just a press of the button makes all commercial transactions feasible irrespective of location. And this technology leveraged to combat social problems including unemployment in most economies.

Insightfully, Kenichi in pages 67-71, postulates the adverse effects inherent in subsidization and protectionism and how disservice these are to consumers especially when the currency of an economy is perceived to be exceedingly strong.

5

It is inspirational for Kenichi to pinpoint the use of internet as 'must have' for one want to be part of the global economy and stipulated the benefits for using internet.

Reviewer's Critique

Kenichi (2002), opined that "the world has become unified and unlike the past, we lived in a truly networked and interdependent world now, with data now passing freely from one side of the world to the other along fibre-optic cables or satellite transmission. Information now defies borders; thanks to information technology that has made this possible".

This assertion by Kenichi is significantly visible in our lives today and this one can strongly subscribe to. The reason being that, first, via information technology educational services like AIU online programmes (distance learning) can be bought by people irrespective of their geographical locations and it is in view of this that I have the opportunity to pursue higher degree at AIU. But for that it would have been extremely beyond my reach since in Ghana such online programmes are alien.

There are innumerable firms that had commercial expediency for adopting E-Tailing, E-Business, M- Management and other electronic forms of doing business and this has enable them to grow to their elastic frontiers. The value in this argument is that it pays to rely on technology and cross borders to compete to be highly competitive in today's turbulent business environment. It is salient to stress that for any country to move out from the economic doldrums information technology will be key, anything short of that will be fiasco since technology breaks borders and enhances enormous opportunities and in the words of Kenichi global economy (information technology) ignores barriers, but if they are not removed they cause distortion

Sight should not be lost on the fact that, Kenichi reiterated the value in individuals, corporations and nations living interdependently for survival and prosperity. A case in point is that, but for the high quality cocoa beans (primary resource/raw materials) from Ghana the western countries would have been found wanting meeting their chocolate preference and Ghana would equally find it increasingly difficult if not impracticable to meet her computer needs. The value here is that Ghana or any of the Western countries do not live in an island but rather interdependently with each supporting the other irrespective of the scale of support. This Kenichi (2005), illustrated by using Riverdance in the Great Hall of the People of China which originated in the Western World, have roots in the Ireland culture with features from other cultures of the world, choreographed by an American and performed in China. This shows how people from diverse background depend on each other for their commom goal and this is a shinning case of interdependency. Considering the fact that China today is the largest holder of U.S. debt, this is just to provide tremendous support to U.S. in its developmental agenda and is a clear case of what independence can do for all economies irrespective of size.

On the contrary, it is imperatively to surmise that due to interdependency nature of economies in the world now, economic, political, social - cultural occurrences (favorable or otherwise) in one country has potential unspecified ramification on others. For example during the global financial crisis, most African countries were disabled seriously in their developmental interventions since grants, aids and even loans were either cut tremendously or were not forth coming or financial commitments pledged to African were not honored, even though this crises had occurred in Europe. The logic therefore is that no single economy is immune from global externalities.

Again, cross-border resource transfers are not a guaranteed recipe for success. For example, "Phillips Electronics sells more colour TVs and DVD recorders in Europe than any other company does; its biggest technological breakthrough was the compact disc. which it invented in 1982. Phillips has worldwide sales of about 38b euros, but as of 2005, it had lost money for 17 consecutive years in its U.S. consumer electronics business. In the United States, the company's colour TV and DVD'S recorders are slow sellers. Phillip notoriously lags in introducing new products into the U.S. market and has been struggling to develop an able sales force that can make inroads with U.S. electronics retailers and change its image as a low-end brand". Thompson et. al. (2007).

Another sour point about cross border business which Kenichi down played is dumping strategies which have the potential of collapsing an economies industry. This runs the high risk of host government retaliation on behalf of adversely affected domestic firms. As a result of liberalization, China for example has in a way dumped the Ghanaian market with all manner of textiles to the extent that the textile industry in Ghana is in dire need of state intervention else it will demise.

It is unpleasant to glorify the second C, Capital as a beneficiary of borderless economy without accentuating its adverse effects on developing economies. This has been exploited by the developed economies in the name global economy and the inevitable is capital flight, to the detriment of poor nations.

Another imperative point worth mentioning is the fact that Kenichi (2005), mooted the idea of empowering the people through decentralization for prosperity and development. This to a larger extent was to enhance borderless economy. For instance in his book "The Next Global Stage", he argued that global economy was in action to the detriment of central planning. This is evident where Regional Governors and bosses in Dalian (China) are encouraged to decide for their future and enhanced implementation of pragmatic policies. To reinforcement this point, Ghana is rigorously decentralizing government operations and this meant empowering the grassroots. People in the grassroots could better identify their needs and provide solution since they better understand their environment than central government. Decentralization enhances possibilities for participation and improves access to services and is the more efficient way of providing public goods.

 Similarly when employees down the lower ladder are empowered to take choices and be responsible for their decision made they perform better than being dictated to.

On the contrary, it appears that in some poor countries with weak institutions and in post conflict situations decentralization has had negative impacts including corruption.

Expenditure decentralization for example may results in local governments suffering from inadequate economies of scale in the provision of public goods; particularly, information and coordination costs may be higher for local governments than for the central government.

Also, if local vested interests are powerful, in the absence of local accountability, decentralization may increase corruption and social fragmentation as well as having the potential to increase the competition and political tensions among local governments. It should be contended that lack of institutional and administrative capacity of local governments may prevent the benefits of decentralization from being realized and coordination problems across different tiers of government may hinder fiscal reforms and implementation of macroeconomic adjustment.

Equally insightful significant point is that Kenichi posited that competitiveness is enhanced by expanding up and adding more common platforms (such as Windows, the Web, English, credit card systems, influential paradigms, and parallel educational backgrounds) whether as a company or as a geographical region. Today, lots of people do business and make lots of money via technology (internet) and payment system is flexible to the extent that by just pressing a button of the key board you are there. This indeed typifies global economy.

Notwithstanding this, Kenichi apart from information technology being a powerful tool did not explore other equally crucial areas that promote global economy like research. This for me is a striking sour point in his book. A shining example is his inability to highlight the dangers in using information technology. Where for example there are rampant fraud associated with the use of credit cards and the ATM's he noted. This has collapsed many businesses and individual prospect rather than enhancing them.

Kenichi's philosophy of visiting a place, meeting with companies, and talking to stake holders is embedded in management by wandering around where a manager interacts with staff, shaking hands with them, observing actions, asking questions, and getting feedback, all this make a manager get a feel of what is actually happening and provides a stimuli to power higher performance from staff.

The lesson learnt in this philosophical remark of Kenichi is that as managers we have to move out of our comfort zones as well as thinking out of the box to explore for immense opportunities. It is desirable to contend that Kenichi rightly hit the point when he postulate that offering subsidies to small holder farmers and complementing it with selective tariffs to protect local producers will defeat the purpose of which these measures are introduced and rather lead to inefficiencies and high cost of living. This will deny any economy from reaping the immerse benefit from global economy. For example in Ghana, the government subsidizes agriculture inputs, with the view to making small holder farmers competitive, rather the subsidize inputs found their way to the neighboring countries through smuggling are sold at relatively higher prices; eventually the rationale for the subsidies is defeated completely.

The bliss with which Kenichi garnished the benefits of using internet as an important component in global economy without pointing the adverse side of internet use leaves much to be desired. He mentioned lower cost, proven safer ways to charge for goods as some of the benefits derived from online shopping. Others included having twenty four hours shopping time online and this is done at consumers and traders own convenience. There is little to think about location and finding items to purchase. There is no risk of traveling and consumers shop at their own convenient time and on any day. Online shopping can be used as a tool to test new products or services.

It is imperative to contend online shopping or E-Tailing has its own associated dangers and if not managed effectively could derail the good intention of the use of it. Notable among them are: users will not have adequate financial security and this may significantly erode the confidence they have in the transaction or the company. This is owing to the fact that cyber crime is on the ascendancy and criminals who are able to access credit and other business cards as well as personal information of consumers can use these to procure products to the detriment of consumers.

It is salient to note that some user will engage in unethical business behavior, crucially the online prices are 'guide prices' and the actual price paid can vary significantly, there could also be item substitution since supermarket websites for instance are not 'real-time', so consumers may order items that are out of stock. When this occurs retailers tend to substitute items that some consumers find woefully inadequate, online services could be used to offload stocks of food close to its best before date and Consumers would have to eat it quickly or throw it away. Equally important point is that the operational efficiencies of the internet could be suspect at certain times especially in developing countries and this could erode the confidence customers repose in business. For instance "there could be slow web response times to inefficient site Coupled with this is the fact that the disposable income of a firm's consumers may be so low that they cannot afford the personal computers, given that they are computer literate and in event where these consumers cannot speak and write English and most website are designed in English, it will be extremely difficult if not impossible for that segment of consumers to transact business with individuals, firms and nations that adopt the global economy if so to speak These adverse effects if not dealt with, will contract sales since some customers may not be interested in conducting business online and the resultant effect will be low profit levels or losses to the companies and this could threaten their very survival.

Kenichi intimated lack of portability from one portal to another as a problem of using E-cards as payment instruments in page 178. It is imperative to state that though Kenichi posited devices that can be used for E commerce settlement, he regrettably did not underscore the substance of Ecommerce in cross border global economy which include:

Context-specific services: E- Commerce makes it possible to offer location based services, which are specific to a given context (e.g. time of the day, location and the interests of the user). Such services offer new opportunities for personalised push-marketing in close proximity to the vendor thereby increasing the probability of sales. It enhances brand presence and thus encourages consumers to remain loyal to brands they are acquainted with.

Time-critical situations: The ubiquity and immediacy of E- Commerce allows the user to perform urgent tasks in an efficient manner, e.g. fast reaction to stock market developments irrespective of his current geographic location. It is also useful in emergency situations.

Spontaneous decisions and needs: Spontaneous needs are not externally triggered and generally involve decisions that do not require a very careful consideration, e.g. purchase decisions involving small amounts of money.

Efficiency increase: E- Commerce helps increase the productivity of the workforce by increasing the efficiency of their daily routines. Time-pressured consumers (employees) can use 'dead spots' in the day, e.g. during the daily travel to and from workplace, more effectively. This can be utilised, e.g. to check e-mails, get current news, order products and carry out bank transactions.

Strengths

It is noteworthy to state that Kenichi credited the works of many business executives and scholars he used to buttress his contention. For instance in his attempt to achieve his aim of explaining what is really happening there in business and politics he relied on business leaders such as Henry Wendt-CEO of Smith Kline Beecham, who saw cross border alliance as a potential savior for America pharmaceutical industry and in the words of Kenichi "His notion of cross border alliances was truly innovative"; Walter Wriston-former Chairman of Citibank, who saw globalization as an imperative not because of management or business theories but because of technological breakthroughs; Akio Morita-co founder of Sony, Kenichi perceived these personalities as being ahead of their time.

It is equally significant to assert that Kenichi's (2005) global economy where borders are dismantled by technology promotes prosperity in all sphere of human life. Quoting Chairman Mao in his Little Red Book from Kenichi (2005) "Today's employees are provided with far better and more interesting facilities. Dalians' shop is stocked with an international range of consumer goods".

One giant material point raised in this book "The next Global Stage" is how marketers can leverage on effective branding and being different in providing superior products that meet the preference of the target market to optimize success. This is a free consultancy service from Kenichi.

It is gratifying to assert that, the book offers entrepreneurs the courage and toolkits to take giant steps to invest beyond their comfort zones and pace their scale up plans since the end results will far exceed their cost of investment.

The numerous editors of the book undoubtedly prove the enormity and quality of arguments in the Book and it further strengthens the point that the Book will stand the test of time.

Weaknesses

A significant egregious in Kenichi's argument of excess liquidity in an economy is that in pages 53-56, he constricted his submission to an advanced nation, positing that when interest rate is deliberately reduced by the economic managers of a nation with the view to making investible funds available for entrepreneurs to invest and expand which creates jobs and trigger demand for commodities since a lot more people now have incomes and can save and the cycle continues on and on and on. This he opined that was rather not the case because of the emergence of global capital market. So the expected investible funds that hither to should have gone to that nation's investors for expansion purposes with its ripple effects as noted above is siphoned out as a result of an attractants (higher interest rate) in other markets across borders.

Alas, this scenario is partly incorrect. For example in developing country like Ghana, there is liquidity overhang according to Bank of Ghana Monetary Policy Release on April 13th, "With respect to money, the Committee observed that since the last quarter of 2011, there has been a substantial liquidity overhang which contributed to a decline in the interbank rates. The lower yield on cedi assets had meant that the excess liquidity was channeled into the foreign exchange market, leading to further depreciation. The foreign exchange pressures are accentuating uncertainties and risking growth. It is the intention of the Bank of Ghana to increase the mopping up of this liquidity and contribute to a reversal of the flight to foreign assets". The logic in this is that the excess liquidity in some cases as noted above find their way to the money market (changing into USD) and not the capital market asserted by Kenichi.

It is detrimental for the book to be silent on policy options for making small holder farmers competitive, since protectionism and subsidization is not the way forward. One would have thought that in expressing dissenting views on these policies (protectionism and subsidization) an alternative like via cross border ventures, farmers cooperative groups will be offered a fair price for their produce that will reflect the social and environmental cost of producing; this will enable smallholder farmers to afford: high yielding input varieties, farm maintenance cost and effective post harvest management cost with the view to maximizing the quality of their produce and enjoying higher productivity which will eventually lead higher income levels. It is when smallholder farmers have fair price for their produce that they can resort to good agronomic practices in production and this will make them more competitive and ensure sustainability in sourcing produce

One strong adverse of Kenichi's book is his inability to highlight vividly the negative effects of resorting to technology and the explosive adverse of deregulating financial markets of countries

To What Extent Has The Book Achieved Its Objective(s)?

For Kenichi to demonstrate with empirical evidence that cross border alliance and business activities offer firms the needed competitive advantage to grow their mark up and build shareholder value. This he illustrated when he proclaimed in page XVIII that a company could build up the best equipped laboratories, staffed with the optimal mixture of experiences and youthful brilliance, it does not guarantee success, since the exponential high overhead cost demands scale up to meet such investment cost. Also Kenichi posited the trade relationship between China and the USA, to illustrate how cross border operations could promote the welfare and programmes of nations. In this case China at the moment is the biggest debt holder of U.S. and this refreshing to the people of U.S.

One objective of Kenichi which his book fulfilled in page XIX is orientating the mindset of business executives and makes them comfortable in their responsibilities as actors on the global stage; this to a greater degree was attained since business leaders that for example accompanied him on his trips round the globe had renewed perspectives on cross border business, his elaborate expatiation on economic theories and their effects on business environment provided a blueprint for businesses, governments, and individuals who intends to thrive in this new environment and the power of technology to create sustainable competitive edge in their respective industry.

It is intriguing to veritable affirm that global economy enormously explains the new life occurring round the world whether it is Finland, Ireland, China among others; and this satisfies the objectives of Kenichi's (2005) book.

Impact of The Book on The Reviewer

The single most influential phrase for in Kenichi (2005), which has gingered people to go all out, is 'In the age of global economy, physical location is much less important. '

The experience of reviewing this book has offered me (and will offer others when they read it) vision and mind-set towards a subject and towards people and built people's self-confidence. This scholarly expedition had set a new base for lifelong learning which will be very useful in the reader's enviable profession. The hard work and profound challenges encountered in the review journey had forged a new disposition in the reviewer. Reading this book, will enable one to gain, since it enables people build original and pertinent dexterities of unraveling strategic issues.

Interestingly, the book provides one with a rich source of knowledge, valuable learning opportunities for one's professional and personal development.

The practical reading and evaluation of the book will present one with immerse prospect to widen and leverage his/her inquiring skills, critical skills, research skills, information management skills, communication skills, management skills, organization skills to construct synergy in problem solving activities.

Ultimately this book appraisal is an intangible dividing line and has gravely equipped me to take advantage of the enormous display of resources from the global environment to help eradicate the current scale of poverty and restrictions.

It is discerning to reveal that the Book has primarily, in most cases armored and in less cases altered my judgment on some concepts Capra discussed, a spotless example is how society brand more affluent people to be flourishing to the height that moral values and principles in creating wealth has been trashed. It should be pointed that I have also profited from some concepts I almost had no knowledge about. It is against this backdrop that I strongly recommend to all and sundry to critically read this Book.

Concluding Remarks

From the above foregoing reasons, fantastic lessons from "The Next Global Stage" indicate that individuals' institutions and nations do not to be rich, in order to become rich; decentralization of decision making leads to growth in more commercial opportunities and not less of power and privileges; the key factor of success is to interact with the rest of the world and operate a borderless economy; visiting a place, meeting with companies, and talking to stake holders shows how you develop a feel for what is going on and constitute arguably the best way of learning; interdependency is the a sure way of survival for all irrespective of ones material position or resources; one should not use geographical location as an excuse for non performance since there are innumerable technologies available to explore for higher performance; information defies physical borders and travel with great precipitation than expected and one has an abundant of data and information to explore for opulence; the use of E-commerce or M-commerce was stressed as useful for today's corporate governance if a firm wants to survive in this turbulent environment; protectionism as a policy to grow indigenous businesses will be a defeatist since the net effect will be rewarding inefficiencies and rather stifle growth.

It will be objectionable to underestimate the value of the thrust of the theme and issues raised by Kenichi inspite of some vulnerabilities identified above in some of his arguments. By and large, this book is not only worth reading but mind boggling.

If according to Kenichi time has eroded the value in Keynes, Adam Smith, David Ricardo and other economic theories in contemporary world; then the greatest question to pose is, will time be a morbid on the value in Kenichi's global economy theory?; only time will tell in the next three, four decades or even less.

By Emmanuel Tete Darko

YOUR KNOWLEDGE HAS VALUE